Why do we have?

ROCKS AND MOUNTAINS

By Claire Llewellyn
Illustrated by Anthony Lewis

BARRON'S

Contents

First edition for the United States and Canada,
published 1995 by Barron's Educational Series, Inc.

First published in Great Britain in 1995 by
Hamlyn Children's Books, an imprint of Reed Children's Books Limited, Michelin House,
81 Fulham Road, London SW3 6RB, and Auckland, Melbourne, Singapore and Toronto.

Text copyright © 1995 by Claire Llewellyn
Illustrations copyright © 1995 by Anthony Lewis

All inquiries should be addressed to: Barron's Educational Series, Inc.,
250 Wireless Boulevard, Hauppauge, New York 11788

International Standard Book Number 0-8120-6524-7 — 0-8120-9394-1 (pbk)

Library of Congress catalog card number: 95-19701

Editor: Veronica Pennycook
Designer: Julia Worth
Consultant: Pat Pye, Ginn & Company Ltd

Printed and bound in China

A Land of Rock

It's fun to scramble over rocks. One moment you're teetering along an edge, the next you're sliding down a shiny slab.

Although we can't always see it, rock makes all the land around us. It lies under fields and hills, and forms the towering mountain peaks.

Beneath your Feet

The ground we stand on is made up of layers. On top there's the soil, where plants grow and worms wriggle. Soil is a mixture of grains of rock and tiny pieces of dead plants and animals that have rotted into the ground.

Beneath the crumbly soil is a layer of heavy clay and stones. And below this lies solid rock.

Inside the Earth

Our planet is not as solid as it seems. Deep inside the Earth, it is so hot that some of the rock has melted; it is thick and runny.

The outside of the Earth is a hard crust. It has cracked in a number of places, into huge pieces called plates.

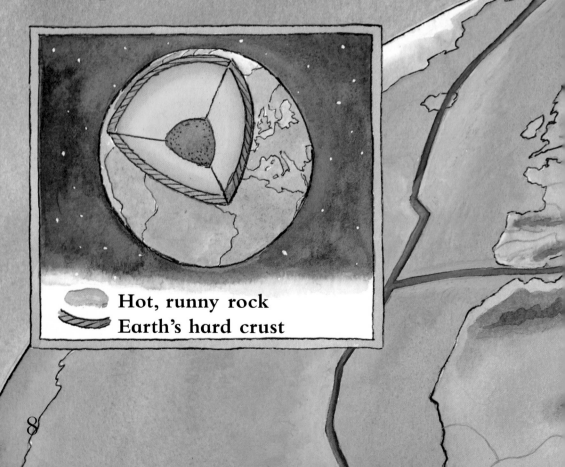

Hot, runny rock
Earth's hard crust

The ground we live on lies on
these plates, which move very
gently on the hot rock below.

The Land Shakes

As they move, the Earth's plates sometimes hit each other. A shock like this can bring complete disaster. The ground trembles, and buildings that once seemed so solid collapse to the ground with a crash. This is an earthquake — and it happens fast.

Moving plate

11

Mountains of Fire

The Earth's crust is thinner in some places than others. The hot runny rock that lies far below can push its way up, and burst out through a crack in the ground. Whoosh! — it's a volcano.

Volcanoes explode like fireworks, hurling out fountains of fiery rock. In time the hot rock hardens, and slowly builds into a beautiful cone-shaped mountain.

Inside a volcano

13

Up in the Mountains

Mountains are magnificent. They tower above the land, far higher and steeper than the hills below.

The craggy peaks stand out against the brilliant sky. They are cold, empty places, beaten by winds and covered with snow and ice the whole year round.

Making Mountains

The Earth's great plates have helped to make mountains. When two plates meet, they sometimes push against each other so hard that the land between them is forced up and squeezed into gigantic folds of rock. This makes a huge row of mountains called a mountain range.

Two plates meet

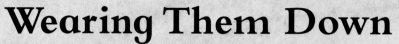

Wearing Them Down

Nothing, not even a mountain, lasts forever. Every day its shape slowly changes. The hard rock is worn away by wind, rain, rivers, and waves, and by the most powerful force of all — moving ice.

This wearing away is called erosion. Over thousands of years, it carves rocks into strange and beautiful shapes.

Rock Building

For millions of years, tiny grains of rock have been carried along in the world's rivers and dropped in the sea. Here, they build up on the seabed, each new layer pressing down on the ones below. The grains were squeezed together so long and so hard that they slowly changed into rock.

← **Rock grains sinking**

Fossils in the Rock

Some of the rock that once formed on the seabed has been pushed up by the Earth's great plates. Now on dry land, it makes the hills and cliffs where we walk and climb.

Hidden in the rock are fossils — the stony remains of long-dead plants and animals. Fossils are like clues. They give us peeks at life from millions of years ago.

Index